LOVING ALL OF ME:
The Inner World

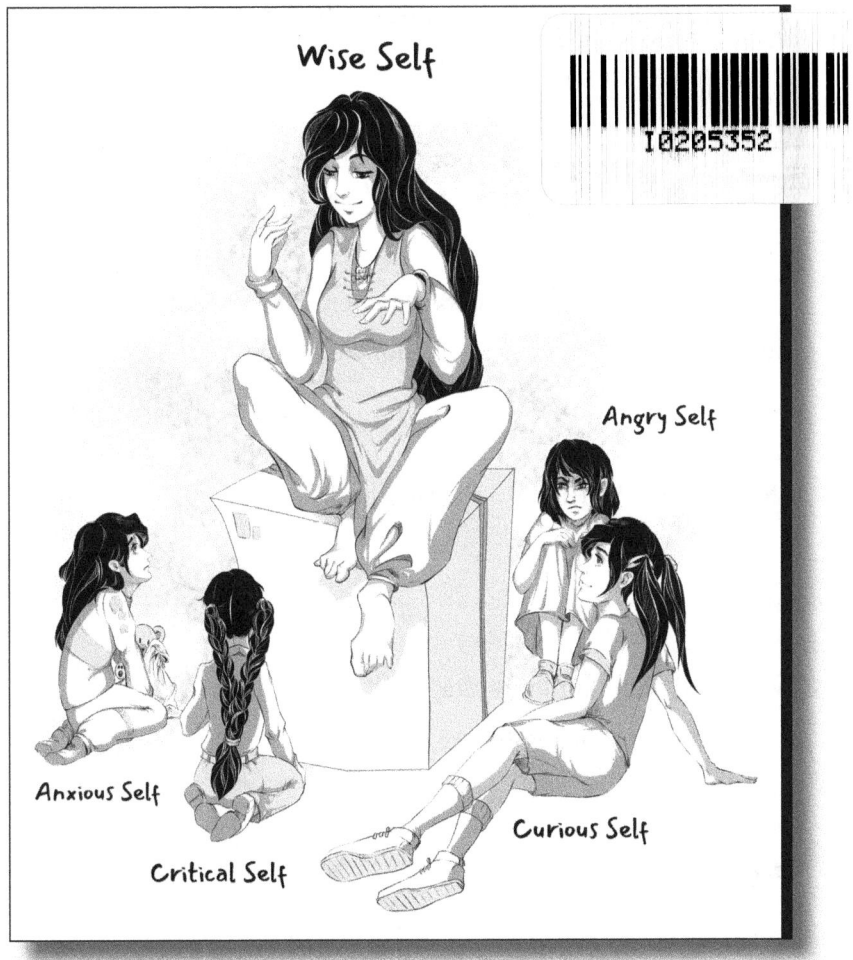

A Guide for Girls of All Ages

Dr. Kimberly Brayman

Illustrated by Irina Denissova

Copyright © 2020 by Dr. Kimberly Brayman

All rights reserved. No part of this publication may be reproduced, stored in a retrieval system, or transmitted in any form or by any means, electronic, mechanical, photocopying, recording, or otherwise, without written permission by the author.

For information regarding permission please write to Dr. Kimberly Brayman at: info@KimberlyBraymanAuthor.com

For bulk and wholesale orders please email Dr. Kimberly Brayman at: info@KimberlyBraymanAuthor.com

ISBN: 978-1-951688-18-9 (paperback)

Written by Dr. Kimberly Brayman
Illustrated by Irina Denissova

First Edition

Team Published with Artistic Warrior
artisticwarrior.com

Dedicated to my children: Chelsea, Kailey and Chad.
You have filled my life with wonder and inspired
me to continue learning what makes us all tick.

This book is designed as a therapeutic guide to help you know yourself better. We've added extra pages at the back of the book for note taking, affirmations and observations.

Loving All of Me: The Inner World

Table of Contents

Chapter One: Know Yourself First 1
Chapter Two: Intro to Soul and Wise Self 7
Chapter Three: Our Inner World 9
Chapter Four: Your Soul 13
Chapter Five: Intuition Is the Gift of the Soul 16
Chapter Six: Our Observer—Wise Self 19
Chapter Seven: Warrior Self 24
Chapter Eight: Storm Troopers 27
Chapter Nine: Emotional Self 29
Chapter Ten: Sexual Self 36
Chapter Eleven: Expressive Self 40
Chapter Twelve: Frazzled Self 43
Chapter Thirteen: Challenging Parts 47
Chapter Fourteen: Boundaries and Protection 50
Chapter Fifteen: Balance 54
Chapter Sixteen: Loving Your Body 57
Chapter Seventeen: Quirky Parts 60

Addendum 62
Notes 63

Coming Soon 71
About the Author 72
About the Illustrator 73

Dr. Kimberly Brayman

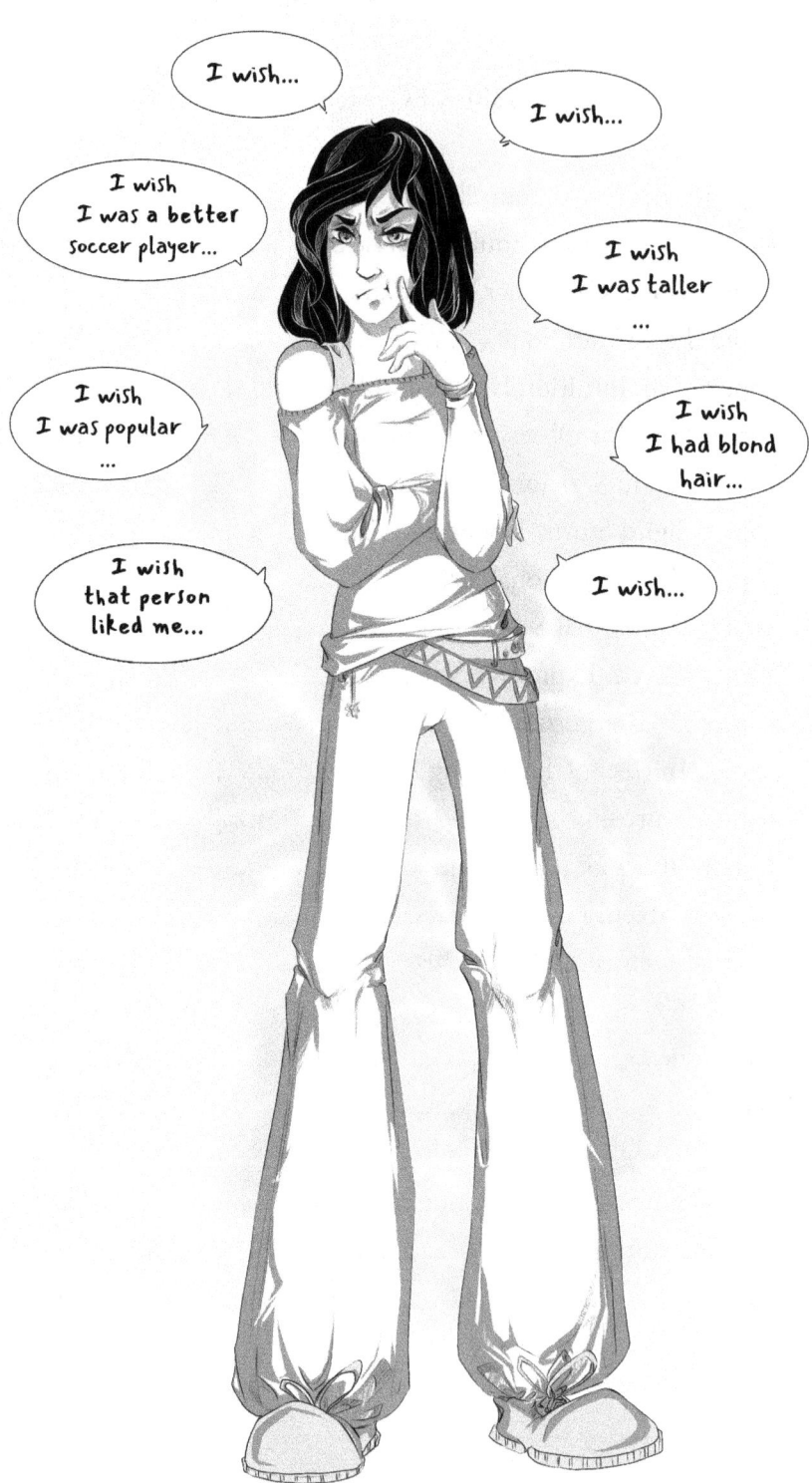

Dissatisfied Self

Chapter One: Know Yourself First

Loving all of yourself might seem a daunting task. Many of you have different characteristics or aspects of yourselves that you wish were different. Some of these things can become goals you choose to work on.

For example: if you practice, you can become better at soccer. There are, however, things you can't change, like how tall you are or what size feet you have.

When you spend time thinking or obsessing about things you can't change, you are throwing away the valuable energy you have for living joyfully and fully.

You need to understand, know and accept yourself as you are before anything else is possible. This guide will help you start at the beginning.

You can spend so much time with your energy directed outward that you forget about yourself in the process. This is more of a challenge for girls. Female neurobiology (your brain) is wired for connection. It's natural for females to be caretakers, friends and, at times, social butterflies. You are wired to be aware of everything going on around you, and you often try to figure out what others need and want. You may try and guess what they are thinking or spend a lot of time trying to understand their intentions.

You can be like a juggler trying to keep all these people and relationships happy. At times, it can feel impossible.

As a girl or woman, you can shift your perspective inwards to learn about yourself first. This allows you to love, guide, support and, yes, sometimes challenge yourself. What can be confusing is there are often different perspectives and competing desires, and this can lead to confusion about what choices to make.

Juggler Girl

Picture your mind as having a unique cast of internal characters who populate your moments. All of them are part of you and it helps to untangle them and understand the different parts that may be trying to run the show. Everyone has a continual dialogue of commentary in their minds.

What can be confusing is that you may have several different perspectives and competing desires. This can lead you to confusion about what choices to make.

Loving All of Me is a guide for your journey. With words, characters and a sprinkling of humor, you may find a rich inner world that will help you understand who you are.

Action Step: Say to yourself, "I will get to know myself because I am awesome and interesting."

Chapter Two: Intro to Soul and Wise Self

As girls and women, you start life with curiosity and a desire to see, touch, hear and live fully. You want to experience the world. You begin with openness and a desire to learn. You are sometimes a whirlwind of excitement and emotion and find it difficult to keep it all together. You are complicated in a wonderful way! It helps to have some strategies to understand yourself and how to work with yourself.

We all have a soul and a wise self. Your soul is your essence, what you feel when you close your eyes and go inside. It is not your body, not your thoughts, and not your feelings. It is the aliveness that peers out of a newborn's eyes, the sense of self you sometimes feel as a woman that is alive and timeless. As an adolescent girl, it may be what you are just beginning to sense beneath all the emotions. It may feel elusive, but it is there.

Your wise self a part of you that you can develop and grow. She develops and learns with you. Whether you listen is another thing entirely. Her job is to see everything you are feeling, thinking and doing. Your wise self observes and can guide you forward. The rest of your parts develop as you do, in fits and starts, in an uneven, unsteady pattern. Some parts may seem younger than others, some older. Some become too loud, and it's difficult to feel balanced. Some develop when you explore and find new things you are passionate about, and some show up to keep you safe. All of your different selves appear for a reason. Your wise self is the one that can be your guide. It is important to hold the idea of the soul and wise self as we go forward in our exploration. It will make sense.

Chapter Three: Our Inner World

Girls and women are amazing, resilient and ever-changing. You are perfect in your imperfections. It is worth restating: you are perfect in your imperfections. After all, you are human, with all the quirks that go along with that. Think how boring it would be if we all looked the same or all liked the same things.

Our differences are what make the world interesting.

Start listening for the different voices in you. Perhaps you can picture how they look; you can certainly hear what they say. Getting to know them will help you understand yourself and help you develop the skill to choose what aspect of yourself handles any given situation. You can learn to soothe yourself when you are upset, encourage yourself when you falter, and become the best that you can be.

You may find many of the things you feel you need from others can be actually be found within yourself. You co-create your life. Life doesn't just happen to you. There are events. You make choices. There are consequences. You are not a victim, although some may choose to play that role. Choose another way, an empowered way. You can, with skill, be an active agent in creating a life you want.

Being an active agent in your life does not mean that bad things never happen. It means you are capable of finding a way to overcome challenges, get past obstacles, and keep moving in the direction that your wise self believes in. As you do this over and over again, you begin to develop a sense of strength, of being capable, and of knowing who you are.

Every aspect of you will announce their views, express their feelings and may even run a little wild in their enthusiasm. Every aspect is there for a reason. Ignoring them, being angry at them, shouting at them, or alternatively letting one aspect run your life, is not going to help.

You have many more internal resources than you may at first believe. You need to learn to notice them, listen to them, access them and help them collaborate to create a life of joy and purpose.

Action Step: An affirmation is a statement that encourages you. Sometimes it helps to write it down on a sticky note and put it where you will see it every day. Examples are:
"I will overcome whatever challenges show up for me"
or "I'm strong and capable"
or "I will learn to help myself in strong and clear ways"
or "I'm little, but I'm mighty".
Write your affirmation here. Use it every day.

_____

_____

_____

_____

_____

Chapter Four: Your Soul

Your soul is the very essence of you—your spirit. You can't see it, but if you close your eyes and go inside, you can feel it. You're not your body. You're not your thoughts and you're not your feelings.

The body is where you live for this lifetime, and your thoughts and feelings are things you experience.

Your soul enters your body when you are born and stays for your lifetime. It simply wants to have a chance to experience life.

Picture your soul as swirling with colors, almost invisible, and beautiful to look at. Everyone has a beautiful soul. You have a beautiful soul.

The Soul

If something incredibly painful happens, it may make you pull away or disconnect from what you are experiencing. You may feel numb or removed from what is happening. This is called dissociation. It's really a way for the soul to protect you if life gets too hard. The soul will look out for you. If it feels like life in general or certain experiences are too hard, it can help to decrease your painful feelings. You will feel more present and aware of the world when your soul feels it's safe for you to experience what's going on.

Sometimes your soul learns to pull away like this when really bad things happen. Sometimes it may not notice when it's safe in your life again. This is okay. If this happens to you, you can work with a therapist and learn how to stay more present. It's like an emergency exit. It's great to have it there, but you likely won't need to use it. If you do use it, you need to come back into the beauty of living fully when it is safe to do so.

Action Step: Think of a time when something really difficult happened and you felt almost like you pulled away from the experience. Write it here.

_____

_____

_____

_____

_____

Talk to someone about it and share how that experience felt at the time.

Example: I fell off the top of a barn when I was much younger. I do not remember falling or landing. I do remember hurting as I came back to the experience of lying there. I do not remember any fear as I fell.

Chapter Five: Intuition Is the Gift of the Soul

The gift that the soul brings is intuition. Girls and women have a strong and very useful intuitive side to them. It can be a gut feeling, an impression. It can be knowledge that is hard to explain in words but you feel is true in your belly or in your bones.

Intuition is the ability to know or understand something instinctively, rather than from learning or thinking about it.

You will know you are listening to your intuition when you simply know something from deep inside you. While you need the ability to think things through, there are other times when your intuition will guide you. Sometimes your intuition will let you know something good is going to happen. One of the main jobs of your intuition is to help keep you safe in the world.

If you have a feeling in your stomach that a situation is not good, or not safe for you, you need to listen. If you are not sure about your intuition you can simply ask, "How does this feel in my body?"

At some point in time your intuition will awaken in you and help guide you. You can thank your soul for guiding you.

> **Action Step:** Think of a situation that is concerning to you and pick one way you could handle it.
> Close your eyes and go inside.
> Ask yourself, "How does handling this in this way feel in my body?"

Chapter Six: Our Observer—Wise Self

Your wise self is a part of you that grows and develops over your lifetime. You can actively make choices that help your wise self develop. The more you ask your wise self for guidance, the more wisdom she gathers—like magic powers that you can access when you need them.

Like the soul, everyone has a wise self bursting with excitement at being part of your life journey. If you don't know where she is, you can start by closing your eyes, going inside and asking, "What would a wise part of me say right now?"

Your wise self may be sleeping, hiding or even bored because you have not been listening to her wisdom. Your wise self needs to be given permission to be your conductor. She respects all of your opinions, loves every part of you—even the parts that are challenging or difficult. Your wise self knows that each part of you is there for a reason and she will never judge you. (A critical part of you might though.) You can learn from your wise self that judging yourself does not make life better.

Everyone is born precious and you need to treat yourself like you would a favorite puppy. We would encourage, love and gently guide that puppy. That is what you need to do for yourself. You are learning as you go.

While everyone makes mistakes, you need to learn from them, make better choices and not be self-critical. You need to admit when you're wrong, or have made a mistake, and then move past it.

This is called taking responsibility for your mistakes. It is a priceless quality to have.

Messy Self

In summary, your wise self is the conductor of your life. She is unfazed by your moods. She simply watches and sees all that you think, feel and do. She holds a calm center, a wise mind. Some people call this your observer or witness space, but, truly, there's wisdom there to be accessed if you listen. If you listen to her, you are on the right path of your life.

The more you listen to the guidance of your wise self, the easier this will be and the clearer her voice will become. She will grow, learn and develop with you. She will also keep track of all the parts of you and choose which one gets to be the main character in that moment of your life. If a part of you is leading the show in an unhelpful way, she can gently ask another part of you to step in and help.

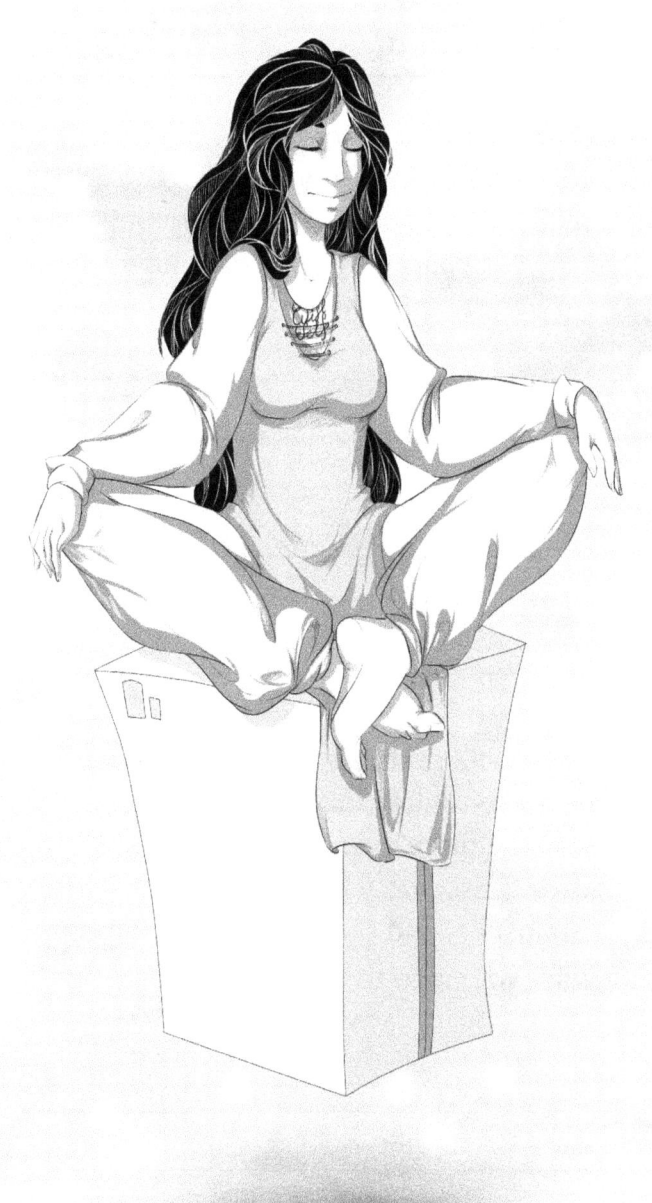

Wise Self

Dr. Kimberly Brayman

Action Step #1: Go inside now and begin a conversation with your wise self. Ask, "Is there anything in life I am trying to figure out? What would the wise part of me say right now?" Write it here.

_____

_____

_____

_____

_____

Action Step #2 : Is there anything that you need to take responsibility for? When you do this, you grow a little more every time. Adults and other kids will also know that you're honest and responsible, and they will trust you more.

Write what you need to take responsibility for here.

_____

_____

_____

_____

_____

Chapter Seven: Warrior Self

The warrior is your brave self. She gifts you with courage and reminds

you that courage and fear can both be present at the same time.

Being afraid is part of life and a sign that you need to keep yourself safe, act swiftly if you are in danger, and triumph stronger than you were before you were challenged.

Sometimes you get a little battered emotionally or physically, but your warrior self can help you move past this. Resilience in life doesn't mean you are never hurt. It means you keep on moving forward with determination. It's how you handle a situation and come through it that matters most. Your warrior self is very proud of you when you get through a big hurt or take a chance and do something even when you are afraid.

Action Step: Is there a time you can think of when your warrior self has helped you out? Remember that fear may have been there too, or tears may have been there, but you made it through the situation and recovered. Write it here.

_____

_____

_____

_____

_____

_____

_____

_____

_____

_____

Chapter Eight: Storm Troopers

So, how are you doing? Let's see. We know that you have a warrior self who gives you courage. She's part of your storm trooper support group: the parts of yourself that help when things aren't going well. We know that in life we need help sometimes. The good news is that while you may have adults to help you, you can develop a strong ability to care for yourself even when you're upset.

There might be a part of you that is good at reminding you to take some slow breaths when you are upset. Visualize this part as a mini-you that sits cross-legged, softens her belly and breathes.

You may have a part of you that knows you need quiet if you feel overstimulated. This could be a part of you that pulls up your hoodie or hides under the covers. Sometimes you may hear her give a huge sigh.

You may have a part of you that just says, "Time to leave this situation. It does not feel safe." This part wants to turn and leave, sometimes without explaining to others.

These are the "How do I rescue myself?" parts. They are part of your storm trooper group that helps calm your internal storms.

Action Step: When you talk to yourself it can make you feel better or worse. Are you offering words of encouragement to yourself?

_____

Are you cooling your upset or adding fuel to the fire?

_____

This awareness of how you talk to yourself is another important step in your development. How can you do better with this?

_____
_____
_____
_____

Chapter Nine: Emotional Self

Everyone has an emotional self, sometimes called your emotional body. You have many emotions and sometimes they may feel too big for your body.

When your emotions get really big, they can spill out of you. This may be tears when you are sad or outbursts when you are angry. It might be a scream of excitement or a sigh of defeat. This is one way you release emotion and you can do this in healthy ways. Crying when you are sad is healthy. Saying mean things when you are angry is not healthy. Talking things out may help you feel better inside. Journaling may help too.

It is necessary to spend some time reflecting so you can learn when and how it's appropriate to express your emotions. At times this part of you might feel very young.

Your emotional body is larger than life, and has a wonderful sense of humor.

Sometimes you may say to yourself, "I feel a little crazy right now." There's no reason to be critical of yourself when this happens. Instead, think of yourself with compassion. Everyone has a lot of emotions. Finding the joy or humor in these scenarios can be cathartic.

There are many feelings . . .

Humorous ENRICHED Elusive Easy-going Insulted Gracious
FRIGHTENED Careless Kindhearted
Terrified Critical Abrasive Effective Alert Afraid Jittery
Intrigued GREAT Cuddly dazzling Fidgety Lability Frustrated
Generous Embarrassed elite Absurd ADVENTUROUS
COURAGEOUS Lost magical Gloomy Committed
Disrespected EMPHATIC Coy FEROCIOUS Flexible
Astounded Ignored Jubilant HESITANT Hated
Challenged BOTHERED Amorous
Agreeable INTENSE Acknowledged Miserable
Gleeful Attractive HORRENDOUS Keen Enabled
Cold-hearted Encouraged Hysterical
Gusty Bossy Delighted Admired Timid Homely
Introverted JAUNTY IRATE Manipulated mean
Gentle Cowardly Disconnected Suspicious
HOSTILE Absorbed Bitter Merry mighty
Fragile ESSENTIAL Absent-minded Disgusting Accepted
Haughty Insistent EXUBERANT Lonesome Forlorn
ECCENTRIC ALARMED CODDLED Dismayed Fearful
Breathtaking Worried COMPASSIONATE
Fearless Compelled Amazing. Graceful Gorgeous Crabby
Guarded Brilliant Gullible Careless Envious Amused
Insensitive ENGROSSED Attentive Broken-hearted Adored
Bratty Energetic Helpful Deserving Helpless
Frazzled Grief-stricken Laughable
Funny furious Flustered Anxious

INTIMIDATED GRUMPY ABANDONED. Happy-go-lucky Deceptive Eloquent emotional Impish FRIENDLY HATEFUL Festive DEPRESSED ASSERTIVE Cheerful Dependable determined Imaginative EDGY Discriminated Enchanted CHIVALROUS Bored ANGRY ANNOYED ABRUPT Ready Healthy Impatient Feisty Fortunate Content Dejected Childlike clever Conscientious Jovial ALONE Appalled argumentative Mediocre Bullied Loving Idealistic ABYSMAL Abusive Mellow CONCERNED Betrayed Crazy Aggressive ambivalent LOATHSOME Overjoyed Doubtful Innocent Compatible Deceived Elegant DEDICATED Melancholy Blissful Messy Adrift Heard Competent Fascinated Important Calm Faint hearted Joyful Humble Homesick Sulky Curious FOOLISH Honest Discouraged Elated JUSTIFIED Hormonal Faithful Docile DISLIKED

Remember that all emotions are a normal part of being human. What you do with them is a responsibility, both to yourself and to those around you. You can learn to be reflective and self-regulating.

To be reflective means you are think about how you behave and how you handle things. It is being aware of what is going on in your emotional body and your thoughts. To self-regulate means you are developing skills to soften or change what you are feeling.

If you don't develop the skills of being reflective and self-regulating, you may not be aware when one emotion becomes too dominant. One emotion can overtake all sense of reason, making your wise self retreat. Your emotions become unbalanced. You're not angry all the time or anxious all the time, but it can feel that way. You might believe that you're only angry or only anxious. These emotions can get so strong they seem to have their own identity.

Action Step #1: You shouldn't harm yourself or another person with your body or your words. Is there a situation you need help handling in a better way? Write it here.

_____
_____
_____
_____
_____
_____
_____
_____

Action Step #2: It is important to remember your emotions are things you experience. They are not who you are. If you feel angry or anxious a lot (or any other dominant feeling), you need to actively look for ways to soothe yourself and feel other emotions. Maybe your silly self can spend some time with a friend or animal, or you can watch a funny video. What dominant emotion(s) do you feel most often?

_____
_____
_____
_____

What other emotions have you felt today?

_____
_____
_____
_____

Chapter Ten: Sexual Self

Every one of us is different in some way from everyone else. We also have many things in common. Sexuality is one area where people have a lot of differences. A person's sexuality is an area that gets a lot of attention, from a lot of people, for a lot of different reasons.

Everyone has an opinion. The reality, however, is that you're attracted to who you're attracted to. That's it. You're the way you are and that's perfectly fine, no matter what anyone tells you. As you grow and develop, sometimes who you are attracted to may change. Sometimes it won't.

You have your own opinion. It may differ from your family or friends. When it comes to complex things like sexuality, it's good to talk to your wise self.

Talk to different people too. Remember, it's your job to be a good human being. That means you respect other people. You make an effort to understand people who are different from you and put your judgement aside. It's all okay. If you are gentle and kind with yourself, you and your wise self will figure this out. It is part of your journey.

All of this is normal. It's your responsibility to make wise choices with your heart and your body. Remember the guidelines that include: "I will respect myself. I will keep myself safe." They apply here.

Also add "I won't do anything today that I might regret tomorrow," and "I will stay away from unsafe situations. If I find myself in an unsafe situation, I will do my best to remove myself from it."

Learning about your heart and body, your sexuality, and the feelings of your heart and body is part of growing up. Making wise choices with your behavior is another.

Action Step: How do you define your sexuality?

_____
_____
_____
_____

Is this clear or unclear?

_____

Changing or constant?

_____

Are you able to be honest about this with yourself?

_____

With others?

_____

Take a breath and let it go.
You will figure this out. It is a process.

Chapter Eleven: Expressive Self

You have wonderful characters who are part of you that need time and room to grow and develop. These parts are creative and curious and full of joy. We must protect them from your critical self, or from the criticism of others.

No one should crush your joy or discourage you from participating in a healthy activity that rejuvenates you.

When you give these parts time and space to simply be, they will grow bright as a shiny star; so bright that others can't dim them. These parts need to be woven into your life regularly and they're helpful when you need to soothe yourself. Give them time to draw, or sing, or dance and you'll feel better. They'll also draw many wonderful feelings out of your emotional self.

Dancer Self

Action Step: What parts of you need room and time to grow?

For example, do you have a dancer self, or an artist self?

Write yours down and make a plan to give them time to grow.

_____
_____
_____
_____
_____
_____
_____
_____
_____
_____
_____
_____
_____
_____
_____
_____

Chapter Twelve: Frazzled Self

There are times you'll feel overwhelmed and out of control. Everyone feels this. There are times you'll feel no one understands you. That's something everyone feels at some time or another.

When you deeply know yourself, you can understand and soothe yourself. This takes time and practice. The next time you are upset, before you reach out to another person, ask yourself, "What can I do that would help me?"

It might be drawing or listening to music or it might be tackling one part of a problem at a time, so that it feels manageable. This is called chunking, and it means breaking a problem apart into smaller sections to work on.

Chunking is one method of handling being overwhelmed. There are times when the right choice is to soothe yourself first, then go back and tackle the life issue that upset you.

Skillful ways to soothe yourself

- Take a bath or shower
- Go for a walk
- Draw
- Write/journal
- Take five slow breaths
- Bake and share cookies, brownies, or a meal
- Call a friend
- Talk to your parents
- Talk to a good adult friend
- Wear an outfit you really like
- Pet your dog, cat or other pet
- Have some quiet time
- Give yourself a pedicure
- Curl up with a good book
- Watch a favorite funny movie
- Take an action step on a problem that is bothering you
- Knit, paint, dance, drum
- Be creative, whatever that looks like for you
- Find something positive to focus on
- Challenge any negative thoughts that arise
- Do a kind thing for someone else (this is really helpful to get out of negativity)
- Do a kind thing for yourself (we underestimate the imortance of our relationship with ourselves)

Action Step #1: How else can you soothe yourself?
_____
_____
_____

Action Step #2: Think about when you feel overwhelmed or out of control.
When does this part of you show up?

_____
_____
_____
_____
_____

Think of a time when you were frazzled.
How did you cope with it then?

_____
_____
_____
_____
_____

How would you cope with it now?

_____
_____
_____
_____
_____

Chapter Thirteen: Challenging Parts

Everyone has parts of themselves they don't like. Do you know the story about the princess who kissed a frog? While the frog may have looked ugly or repulsive on the outside, she saw there was something worth loving. She kissed the frog and found something magical. The parts of yourself that you don't like are like that frog.

They need to be listened to and loved, and sometimes a part of you that seems ugly will turn out to be valued.

At times these challenging parts shout and you may need to let them calm down before you can really understand them. If you don't listen to them, you won't know what they need or what they are doing. They may also help you when you least expect it.

Sometimes these parts think blaming others will help you feel better. Remember that you're responsible for how you feel and how you handle things. Your wise self won't always let these parts have their way, but it will listen so that you can help them.

We all deserve to get help and support. It's sometimes hard for someone else to know what you need help with. While you may get an adult to help you, there are many times you can help yourself.

Action Step: What other parts of you are you aware of? Write them here.

_____
_____
_____
_____
_____
_____
_____

How do they help you?

_____
_____
_____
_____
_____
_____

Chapter Fourteen:
Boundaries and Protection

We need to remember that warriors, and other emotional parts, are there to protect you. Sometimes people say you shouldn't be angry, but anger can be helpful too.

Learning to set boundaries is an important part of keeping yourself safe. Boundaries are like roadblocks that you put up for a purpose. They may be boundaries you set up inside or outside of yourself. Sometimes you speak softly when you set boundaries. If you are too soft, your warrior self may get louder.

Your responsible self can help you choose. For example, you may have a class early tomorrow, but you want to stay up until 3:00 am to watch videos. Instead, you sent a boundary within yourself that says you need to go to bed by 11:00 pm to be alert for class the next day.

Boundaries are a lot about how you set limits with yourself and with other people. They're also how you protect yourself. A good boundary to set is to always be truthful. Even if someone else wouldn't know if you lied, you would know. You can call this a boundary or a value. It's a line in the sand you choose not to cross.

Another example might be saying no to drugs. You have to set that boundary for yourself first. You have to decide who you want to be. Do you want to be someone who cultivates and finds joy in healthy ways? Listen to your wise and responsible selves when these questions come up.

Sure, someone might offer you drugs or encourage you to use them. If you have already set a clear boundary with yourself, it's much easier to set that boundary with other people.

Another example might be someone who wants to touch you in ways that make you uncomfortable. You need to say, "No," and say it strongly. You can set a boundary that says you'll do your best to not allow others to touch you in ways you don't want. It may be hard to do this, but the best thing you can do for yourself is try.

To recap: a boundary is a line in the sand, a stop sign, a clear way for you to think about a situation. Your job is to let your actions back that up. It's much harder to do this with someone who is older, someone in a position of power or authority, or someone you want to like you. You really have to think about these situations. You shouldn't do things or allow things to try and get someone to like or approve of you. You're more valuable than that. People who have your best interests at heart won't try and coerce you into making poor choices or choices against your will.

If you are the one who is tempted to make a poor choice, sit down and have a discussion with your wise self. Think again.

Action Step #1: What is a situation with yourself where you need to set boundaries? Is there something you are tempted to do that you know you should not? Write it here.

_____
_____
_____
_____
_____

Set an affirmation that encourages you to set a limit or boundary.

_____
_____

Action Step #2: Have you been in a situation where you need to protect yourself by setting boundaries or limits? If so, when?

_____
_____

What happened?

_____
_____

If you cannot sort this out yourself, go talk to someone you trust now.

Chapter Fifteen: Balance

Balance in life is a little like walking a tightrope wire above a canyon full of obstacles. If you fall in, you could be swallowed up in your own anger, or be stressed and overwhelmed. This can happen if you don't give yourself time to rest and time to be creative. You need to keep subtly shifting to stay in balance. When you feel yourself out of balance, your first priority is to return to a place of balance.

Remember that everyone gets out of balance sometimes and some parts of you get too big or too loud. It may take a while, but if you love what you feel are your unlikeable parts, they will get smaller and you will be more balanced. Loving them is like shining enough light into the darkness until the darkness is light.

Much of this book is about how to help yourself return to balance. It's about learning to self-reflect and self-regulate and how this can bring you back into balance.

Set aside time to be creative as this can help bring you back into balance. Learning to love yourself and treat yourself with kindness and humor brings you back into balance.

When you push yourself to keep going and you're feeling overwhelmed, tired or upset, it rarely works. Find small moments to bring yourself back to balance.

So often we hear from girls, women and ourselves, "I just don't have the time." When you hear yourself saying these words, it's time to take a belly breath.

Take a deep breath into the bottom of your belly and slowly exhale. Then take a moment to look for something beautiful. You can always carve out a moment to think of something you are grateful for. You can always find a moment to make yourself the priority.

Action Step #1: Soften your belly.
Take one slow breath.

Now, look for something beautiful
and take a moment to appreciate it.

Action Step #2:
Write one thing you are grateful for today.
_____
_____
_____
_____
_____
_____

Repeat this affirmation aloud to yourself:
I am important and will work on balance every day.

What other affirmation can you say aloud to help keep yourself in balance? Write it here:
_____
_____
_____
_____
_____
_____

It is important to get a notebook and write about gratitude every day. When you think of other positive affirmations, write them down too.

Chapter Sixteen: Loving Your Body

Think about how precious your one and only body is. You need to nurture this relationship. For many girls and women, it can be a challenging one. You can let your critical self have a big voice instead of accepting yourself for how you were made. Or you can help your body be as healthy, capable and strong as it can be.

Your body can change throughout your lifetime and sometimes it can be confusing, sometimes exciting, sometimes scary, and sometimes exhilarating.

Here are a set of guidelines for you to look after your body.

Action Step #1: What feelings do you have about your body? Write them here.

_____
_____
_____
_____
_____
_____
_____
_____
_____
_____
_____
_____
_____
_____

Action Step #2: What will you do to have a good relationship with your body? What healthy goals do you have, or do you want to set? Is there a new sport or a new activity that you would like to learn? Write it here:

_____
_____
_____
_____
_____
_____
_____

Action Step #3: Are there any things you are doing with your body or things you are saying about your body that you would like to change?

_____
_____
_____

Set another affirmation for yourself and write it on a sticky note. It could be something like: "I'm going to appreciate the body I have" or "I'm going to help my body grow strong." You can also write your affirmation here:

_____
_____
_____

Chapter Seventeen: Quirky Parts

Everyone has quirky parts. These are any special, unusual, or well-loved parts of you. What do you love to do? It may be a part of you that is simply crazy in love with one thing.

There are girls who know about the vast world of Pokemon or anime. There are girls who love fantasy novels. There are girls who love to write novels. Sometimes, your quirky parts can grow into your strongest attributes.

What quirky parts do you have?

_____
_____
_____
_____
_____
_____
_____
_____

What do you love about those quirky parts?

_____
_____
_____
_____
_____
_____

In getting to know yourself, try and work with these guidelines.
- Listen to all the parts of you. They are all there for a reason.
- Let your wise self guide you when you are unsure.
- Help yourself first, and then if you need to, ask someone else for help.
- Don't listen to the critic. Your wise self will guide you.
- There is no place in loving yourself for being mean, insulting or cruel.
- Make time in your life for the parts of you that bring you joy.
- Learn how to calm and soothe yourself by asking other parts of yourself for help.
- Never physically hurt yourself.

I am amazing just the way I am!

Addendum

This book is a starting point for identity work. It's also a jumping-off point for discussion. Until you know and understand yourself, you can easily get lost in the social labyrinth.

This guide will help identify areas that girls need to work on, or areas of challenge. It also should be affirming and normalizing, and identify creative aspects for girls and women who want more of a balanced life. It's about identifying what is awesome or could be awesome in that life.

We, as girls and women, need to identify with our multifaceted nature and develop a positive self-concept.

We can be perfect in our imperfections.

We are complicated.

We are interesting.

We are awesome.

This is but a moment in your lifelong journey of growth. I'm right here, cheering you on!

Dr. Kimberly

Notes

Write any other thoughts you have here.

Coming Soon

Loving All of Me: The Outer World and *Loving All of Me: A Group Facilitator's Guide,* a guide for group work, will be available shortly.

There are also two wonderful stories coming soon about helping to save the planet. Set in a not-to-distant future, *Brothers of the Earth* and *Sisters of the Earth* are perfect for the super reader or young adult reader. They are sure to entertain and educate all at the same time.

For updates on when books are available visit the author's website at: kimberlybraymanauthor.com.

About the Author

Dr. Kimberly Brayman is a licensed psychologist and has spent decades working in health care. She's inspired to build confidence, normalize struggle and inspire hope through books that build empathy and empower the reader to find their own self-reliance and strength. She believes that we are all complex, emotional and multifaceted beings.

Dr. Brayman has spent decades living, studying, traveling, and working/volunteering in the health care system. She has many interests and is a harpist, an artist, a country and ballroom dancer, a lover of life, and a woman who is determined to live fully with an open heart. She and her five siblings have crisscrossed the globe. She has three adult children who live in China, the United States and Canada. They work in education, health care and the Canadian military and all carry core values of healing and of wanting to make the world a better place.

For several decades, Dr. Brayman has believed in resilience, healing, and the capacity of people to rise from obstacles and challenges and move forward, as slowly or quickly as that may be. Her life's passion is to understand and facilitate the growth and development of girls and women.

Dr. Kimberly Brayman is a registered psychologist (registration #2464) in British Columbia, Canada and until 2020 was also a licensed psychologist in Colorado, USA.

About the Illustrator

Irina Denissova loves creating illustrations for children's books. Her creative talents bring a magical atmosphere to stories, making them enjoyable for both parents and children. She believes the best part about being an illustrator is that she helps create new worlds for readers to explore.

She lives in Temirtau, Kazakhstan and, in her spare time, loves to read and create whatever drawings pop into her mind.

Dr. Kimberly Brayman describes her as a humble, unbelievably talented young woman who has a near-magical ability to take her descriptions and characters and create what she sees in her mind.

Illustrated Children's Books by Dr. Kimberly Brayman

Nana Loves You More
Artsy Alphabet
Count With Me
Blueberries
Atreus and the Fisherman

Young Readers Chapter Books by Dr. Kimberly Brayman

Avry's Magical Cat: A Marshmallow the Magic Cat Adventure
Avry adopts a magical cat from the animal shelter and discovers he is magical like her Nana. Available on Amazon.

A Troll in the Woods: A Marshmallow the Magic Cat Adventure
A true quest that shows courage and fear can go hand in hand, and the power of friendship to inspire action. Available on Amazon.

Avry & Atreus Save Christmas: A Marshmallow the Magic Cat Adventure
A delightful Christmas tale to be read every holiday season. Available Christmas 2020.

Marshmallow Paints the Town: A Marshmallow the Magic Cat Adventure
A fun story that focuses on collaboration, self-responsibility, making mistakes and recovering. Coming Soon.

A Trip to the Hot Springs: A Marshmallow the Magic Cat Adventure
A lovely story with a focus on friendship, magic, and skills to assist with anxiety. Coming Soon.

Nature focused adventure chapter books for tween & teen readers.
Brothers of the Earth
Sisters of the Earth
These books, set in the future, examine the relationship we have with the world around us and highlights external and internal conflicts.

Get up-to-date information on current books, books coming out soon, and books being written.

Follow Dr. Kimberly Brayman's blog on her website at kimberlybraymanauthor.com/blog.

www.ingramcontent.com/pod-product-compliance
Lightning Source LLC
Chambersburg PA
CBHW070208100426
42743CB00013B/3097